Simple Acts of Moving Forward

PRAISE FOR

Simple Acts of Moving Forward

"This astonishing volume is full of simple things to do right now to keep us moving forward when it feels impossible to take another step. Even implementing one or two of these small acts can change your life."

—Cindy Crosby, author of *By Willoway Brook*

"Every once in a while, a profound little book comes along that helps us uncomplicate our lives. *Simple Acts of Moving Forward* is such a book. As you read this stunningly simple volume of little steps, you will find yourself saying, 'Hey, I can do that!' That's because you can."

—John Fischer, author of *Finding God Where You Least Expect Him*

Simple Acts of Moving Forward

60 SUGGESTIONS FOR GETTING UNSTUCK

VINITA HAMPTON WRIGHT

LOYOLAPRESS.
A JESUIT MINISTRY
Chicago

LOYOLA PRESS.
A JESUIT MINISTRY

3441 N. Ashland Avenue
Chicago, Illinois 60657
(800) 621-1008
www.loyolapress.com

This is a revised and updated version of *Simple Acts of Moving Forward: A Little Book about Getting Unstuck* originally published in hardcover in 2003 by Random House / Waterbrook (ISBN 0-87788-082-4).

Cover image © PM Images/Getty Images
Cover design by Judine O'Shea
Interior design by Maggie Hong

Library of Congress Cataloging-in-Publication Data
Wright, Vinita Hampton, 1958-
 Simple acts of moving forward : 60 suggestions for getting unstuck / Vinita Hampton Wright.
  p. cm.
 Originally published: Colorado Springs, Colo. : Shaw Books, 2003.
 ISBN-13: 978-0-8294-2812-4
 ISBN-10: 0-8294-2812-7
 1. Self-actualization (Psychology)—Religious aspects—Christianity. 2. Self-actualization (Psychology)--Prayers and devotions. I. Title.
 BV4598.2.W75 2009
 158.1—dc22

                                                      2008036243

Printed in the United States of America
09 10 11 12 13 Versa 10 9 8 7 6 5 4 3 2 1

To the scores of people who, unawares,
have instructed, nurtured, and encouraged me.

CONTENTS

Acts of Generosity

Acts of Healing

Acts of Integrity

Acts of Joy

GETTING UNSTUCK, MOVING FORWARD, FEELING BETTER

Most of us work hard, and we mean well. But we get stuck. And we get hung up, not on the big things or the months and years, but on the small things that make up our single days and hours.

You may have larger dreams for your life, but your most common struggles have to do with what you're doing today, during this small collection of moments. You've probably been forward-thinking enough to make plans, and you're doing your best to make them happen. But even the best efforts don't always satisfy you—and, too often, you beat yourself up for that. Sometimes you feel that you will never get ahead or even get beyond the spot you're in right now.

The only way to get unstuck is to take a step. It can be a big or little step, and you usually have a choice of directions. But it's an action with purpose behind it, and no one else can do it for you.

Moment by moment you and I are making decisions and taking actions that help us move through time. Sometimes we move ahead in survival mode, "making it" but just barely, and not in a way that feels positive or successful. Occasionally, we slip backward or make choices that undo some of our progress. And sometimes we move in a way that is meaningful and gives us a feeling of forward motion.

This little book is for helping that forward motion. You can dip into the sections in no particular order. They describe sixty powerful acts that can make the difference in your hour, your day, maybe even your life. Some of these acts are easier than others, but they are all possible, and they will definitely move you forward. One simple act is a step in the right direction.

It won't take longer than five minutes to read any one suggestion in this book. And in many cases, it won't take longer than a few minutes to actually take the step. Some steps will lead you to carve out larger blocks of time, such as an afternoon activity or a weekend trip. But the majority of these acts are designed so you can do them immediately. Their purpose is to help you get unstuck from right where you are.

At the end of each act is a short prayer to help you, if you so choose, reach out to God for the love, wisdom, and power that are beyond your own abilities. After the prayer is some space, in case you want to make a note to yourself. If you follow through and do a simple act of moving forward, you might just want to celebrate by writing down what you did.

Read these acts one at a time. Be kind to yourself. And be kind to all the other folks who are trying to take those forward steps as well. Journey with them when you can. A step at a time, in good company, will make us all feel a lot better.

Acts of Creativity

Creativity opens us to revelation, and when our high
creativity is lowered . . . so is our capacity to see angels,
to walk on water, to talk to unicorns.

MADELEINE L'ENGLE,
MADELEINE L'ENGLE HERSELF

Make a List

Jump Ahead Ten Years

Think Again

Write Your Story

Find the Child

Reorder Your Universe

Imagine the Worst

Put Yourself in the Divine Story

Leave the Box

Take a Road Trip

MAKE A LIST

There's so much to do that I don't know where to start. I think of everything I'm responsible for and everything I'd like to accomplish, and I panic—and sometimes I cope by doing nothing at all.

When life gets cluttered, get a huge sketchpad and just list everything you can think of that needs your attention. You don't write anything in order of importance or difficulty; you just get it down so you can look at it. Then you move to another sheet of paper and start sorting the mess on the first sheet and throwing the items in some loose order onto the second. You categorize however you want. Maybe one list is "urgent," another one is "fun," another is "people I need to spend time with." The beauty of lists is that you can work with them so they serve you.

And it is important that your list serve you, not the other way around. When used well, lists can help you collect yourself. But they can beat you up when you give them undue power. You have to decide when it's time—or not time—for a list. You have to decide what kind of list it will be and what power you will give it.

Sometimes you might make a list of all the tasks that need to be done—every last one—just so you can give yourself permission to cross out half of them and not worry about those. Or maybe you put that half on another list to be dealt with later. In doing that, you have relieved yourself, for today, of those tasks and narrowed today's list to something that is doable.

Lists are good for dreaming, for prioritizing, for helping the mind make order out of a situation that has become overwhelming. Not every person enjoys lists. In fact, a list for me is a somewhat left-brained, straight-lined thing. Another sort of person might cut that sheet of paper into little pieces, each piece with one task written on it, put those pieces of paper in a jar, and then draw out an item for the day and go from there.

But when you make a list—when you take what's on your mind and put it out where you can see it, handle it, and do with it as you please—you regain some control over a mind gone berserk with clutter and worry. A list can be very helpful this way. The key is to never allow the list to be the boss. I no longer expect to tick off everything on a list. It's a mere tool, something to help me keep my place, to keep track of life's details.

A Little Prayer for the Next Step

I can't control most of what happens in life, but right now I can write down what's on my mind and give it some order. Thank you for the ability to make lists. I ask that they would serve me well as I seek more order and calm in my life.

JUMP AHEAD
TEN YEARS

*I am stuck, stuck, stuck. I don't want to be doing
this. I'm sick of this project. I think I may actually
be sick of my life.*

When the details of a given day or week get to be frustrating or
discouraging, ask yourself, What do I want to be doing—and
who do I want to be—ten years from now? Dare to write down
the first thing that comes to mind. Then have the courage to look
at your life. Are your present activities leading you to the person
you want to be in ten years? If not, don't panic. Give yourself
permission to *be* dissatisfied with what you're doing now. Go
ahead and imagine quitting the current thing and looking for
something else that would set you on the better path.

Allow the ten-years-ahead vision to release you from today's
anxiety. If you look carefully at your present tasks and worries,
you may see that few of them have any long-term value to you.

If you don't succeed at this class or project, how important is that? On the other hand, if you hope to be married to this same person ten years from now, what can you do today to keep the relationship healthy? If you believe you have gifts that aren't getting any exercise now, what can you begin to do—even in small increments—to make room for those gifts in your life?

I knew I would change to a writing career a few years before I could make the shift in terms of my job. But the day I knew what ten-years-ahead should look like, I began to make plans and take steps, some of them pretty small. The vision helped me persevere, and it eventually led me to a second career.

The ten-years-ahead vision is good for clarifying what's important. It also can remind you of what your true purpose or your real dream is, and it just might give you the courage to take a step toward it. Of course, any such vision is speculation, but long-term dreaming can help you focus better on today and persevere in—or step away from—the present job or project. Our culture does not teach us to think in the long term; political plans often aim merely for the next election, and corporate plans tend to address only this year's urgent issues. But creative people learn to step back and think forward regularly, to keep life fresh, to view larger options, and to give themselves inspiration.

A Little Prayer for the Next Step

Help me think bigger and more long term. Life goes by quickly, and I don't want to get bogged down in details that won't matter even a month from now. I offer you my anxiety in exchange for creative dreams for my life.

Act 3

THINK AGAIN

How did this project ever get so bogged down? Why won't it work? Where's the inspiration? Where's the punch? I should be doing better work than this.

Don't assume that you've thought through anything completely. There's always an angle you haven't considered or data you haven't computed.

So if the given task is not going well, just stop. Back away from the thing however you can. Get up from your desk, if that's where you work, and step away from that computer screen or spreadsheet. Turn around a few times (yes, physically turn yourself around). Take some deep breaths. Sit in a different place or in a different position. Find a pen in a different color of ink.

And think again. Instead of starting where you left off, take up the thread of thought at a completely different place. If you're at the beginning, look at the end. If you're stuck in the middle, remember the beginning that inspired the whole thing.

When my fiction writing bogs down, I switch from creative and intuitive thinking to working on time lines or doing research—or even doing a spell check. One friend of mine shifts to writing with her nondominant hand when she's stuck.

Shift modes and ideas. Ask yourself what you're assuming to be the goal, the problem, or the main part of the process. Ask yourself what you're assuming to be true and false, good and bad.

You always have more brain cells than you're currently using. So exert a few more of them and think all over again. If you do this often, you will become known as a genius simply because you thought about something one more time.

A Little Prayer for the Next Step

Okay, so what am I missing? Where's the puzzle piece, the new approach, the right angle? I'm going to try again, but I need your help.

Act 4

WRITE YOUR STORY

*I'm so tired of my own problems, my bad memories,
and my weaknesses as a person. I'd love to be
another person entirely, to get rid of some of
this stuff. But you can't undo the past, can you?
I guess I'm stuck with myself.*

How you think about yourself influences how you act, so it's in everybody's best interests that your self-image be healthy.

Today find a quiet place and take fifteen minutes to write the story of your life. That's right—just fifteen minutes to cover your whole life. Write quickly so you can't think much about it. You may be surprised at the choices you make when you have only a few minutes to summarize your life.

Read what you've written. What stands out? What important things were left out? Are there any surprises? What makes you feel good, or not?

Now you're ready to write about your life a few more times. You can do this today or spread out the process over several days

9

or weeks. Every time you write your story, choose a different part of it to emphasize. Concentrate on a certain period of your life. Or write only about turning points, failures, accomplishments, friendships, losses, or employment. Each time you write, do it quickly and for only fifteen minutes.

Years ago I read a book about writing biographies, and it stated that the best biographies do not recount a person's life chronologically or merely provide facts but are organized around a theme that emerges from the person's life. A good biographer edits out what does not serve the theme. Even the person's weaknesses and mistakes are presented in the context of that theme. And some material is extraneous and doesn't need to appear at all.

You will discover that your life story contains many extraneous details. Life is multilayered, and not one but several themes will emerge as you explore your history. You cannot undo hurtful events, but you can rethink them in the context of your life themes. You can even decide that, in the overall scheme, certain events are not as important as you have allowed them to be up to now. And you can use the raw material of your history to create a theme for the rest of your story, starting today.

A Little Prayer for the Next Step

Show me my life in different ways. Help me feel free enough to pick and choose the events I want to emphasize and write about. Show me the themes in my life, as well as the gifts, the successes, and the times I've been truly happy.

Act 5

FIND THE CHILD

*Sometimes I feel so needy. It's embarrassing
how much I crave attention and how much I
hope for others' affection and signs of approval.
When will I learn to be a grownup?*

Sometimes you need to pay attention to the small person who still resides in your soul. You can't approach that person with the usual adult solutions. Forget the normal pep talk you give yourself when you need to push through the week. Walk right on by your favorite junk food or libation that the adult so often turns to for comfort. No, today you're going to pay attention to the child who still lives inside you. And that child needs a much more basic kind of help.

Search out any image or record of yourself as a small child. Look for pictures, items from grammar school, references about you from other people's letters or photo albums. Find old toys and books.

If at all possible, go to places you treasured as a child—a tree in your grandmother's yard, the softball field at the junior high school, the indoor and outdoor spaces where you could play without being bothered by adults.

What did you really love to do as a child? What kind of people did you admire? Who scared you, or who could always make you feel better? What were your favorite foods, television shows, games, books?

Immerse yourself in that little person you were back then. Look at her picture and pretend that you've never seen this child before. Try to see what she needs, what she fears, what she dreams about.

Now, write that child a letter—to give her courage and happiness and hope. Tell her precisely how beautiful and smart and interesting she is. Tell her that God is really excited to have her life unfold on planet Earth.

A Little Prayer for the Next Step

You know that I've not been too forgiving or accepting of the me who was a child once. I've tried to grow up and leave that person behind. But the child is still in here, needing love and encouragement. Thank you for giving me a fresh look at this wonderful little person. Show me how to love her better.

Act 6

REORDER YOUR
UNIVERSE

*My life feels so numb, so immovable. I wake up,
and today is just another version of yesterday.
What am I doing, anyway?*

My grandma rearranged the furniture every few months. She totally repainted things about that often too. In the earlier years of her marriage, she and Grandpa moved a lot, right in the same town, first to this house and then another, fixing up each one during residency.

Grandpa's thing was cars. We found a note he'd written to himself long ago, recording that he'd bought and sold seventy-two cars that year.

Some people change jobs often; others switch roommates. But if you're not into drastic changes, smaller ones will do. Sometimes all it takes is a new tablecloth to reorder your universe. Or a new desk organizer. Some writers can start all over again when we buy a new pen and journal.

Every now and then, change things. Buy a new backpack or reorganize your DVDs. Eat dinner in a different part of your house. Change what you've hung on the walls. Make a shift in one or two large items on your schedule. Even a small change can be enough shock to your system that you'll be forced to take some deeper breaths. It will give your creativity a chance to stretch its legs.

Find one thing to do this very day that will disrupt your little universe. Stability is a good thing, but stagnation is not.

A Little Prayer for the Next Step

Please help me rearrange the structure that holds me and controls what I do and how. Help me do at least one thing that changes the order of things. Help me experience the freedom I have to make choices that will help life feel more hopeful and new.

Act 7

IMAGINE THE WORST

*Worry is invading everything I do. I feel all revved up
inside, as if I'm getting ready for something awful to
happen. But I don't know what that awful thing is. I just
feel it—through every hour, every conversation. Without
realizing it, I'm clenching my fists and gulping for air.*

Go ahead. Imagine the worst thing that could happen right
now—the person who could die or the possession that could be
lost or destroyed or the job that could end or the relationship
that could change. Imagine it in full color, in vivid detail.

Now, imagine yourself coping with that worst-case sce-
nario. At first, "coping" may consist entirely of crying a lot and
throwing things. But, hey, that *is* coping, or part of it. So imagine long days of crying and being unable to do much. Imagine
days and weeks of that if you must. Then imagine what you
would do after the tears and depression have subsided. See yourself moving forward another step. See yourself making another
start entirely—finding a completely new job or meeting new

people who accept you as you are. See yourself taking time out of your difficult life to go somewhere more peaceful. See yourself sleeping as much as you need to and then getting the energy required for what comes next.

No matter what happens today or tomorrow, there will always be more options than are immediately visible. You have just imagined a number of them. If your imagination is strong enough and smart enough to get you through your imaginary trials, think of how much better equipped the *whole* you is for getting through The Worst That Can Happen.

See, you can handle whatever comes. So put the anxiety and fear away, at least for the remainder of today.

A Little Prayer for the Next Step

I am so afraid of all the bad things that might happen. There are no guarantees. Everyone is visited by tragedy, and no one is ever really "ready" when it happens. Help me have faith in the ability you've already placed inside me to get through tough times, to help me start over and remake my whole life if necessary.

Act 8

PUT YOURSELF IN THE DIVINE STORY

*I can't believe I looked through every shelf in the DVD
rental store and couldn't find a single movie I wanted
to watch. Nothing in my own home interests me.
Am I dead or just bored?*

When life gets stale and boring, it helps if you remember that by simply existing on this planet, you play a part in a story that is much bigger than your particular plotline. Mystics and other spiritual pioneers have understood this and were thus able to appreciate the dailiness of life as having a deeper significance than was immediately apparent. Every small thing you do today will either make the world a richer place or a more toxic one.

So stand back from your day, and try to see yourself as a person living the divine drama. Imagine the people who have been here before you—yes, here in this house, in this town or neighborhood. Imagine those who will live here after you are gone. Consider the work you do and how that matters beyond your time and paycheck. Meditate on all the words you will speak today and how they will move you forward or others forward—or not.

You might even write your part of the grand story line. Find a pen you like, or settle down at the computer, and compose a work with this title: My Story of This Day. Dare to write this at the beginning of the day, anticipating what might happen. Or write it at the end of the day as a sort of review. Look for the underlying conflicts that keep your plot interesting. Explore the fears, desires, and other motivations that cause you to get up in the morning and do the things you do. Pay attention to the details of other characters and the subplots they contribute.

If you attend to the story of your quite significant life, it won't matter so much that you leave the movie store empty-handed. In fact, that may be a sign that your own plot needs more attention, and applause.

A Little Prayer for the Next Step

Some days it's hard for me to believe I even have a story. Help me see it. Help me live it as though it were truly important.

Act 9
LEAVE THE BOX

People probably think I'm a real bore because I'm never interested in doing anything new. Maybe I am a bore. But it's scary doing new things.

Today you're going to do what you never do. You're leaving the box that you believe is everyone's perception of you. You're leaving your own perception of you. Today you're someone a little bit different. You go someplace you've never visited. You wear a bright color of lipstick—or none at all. Or you buy a jersey of the hometown team and go to a game. You hang out with people who have invited you several times, but you never took them up on it. Someone says, "You want to drive out to antique county for a day?" and you go along, even though you can live without old pieces of furniture that are beyond your budget.

When I was first dating the man who would become my husband, I went to a Super Bowl party with him. I have never connected with football in any positive way. Jim doesn't care for it that much either, but here was an opportunity to hang out with some friends on a Sunday afternoon.

No, I didn't become a football convert. But I participated in the banter (and, of course, in the eating and drinking), and later I turned the experience into a humorous piece for journalism class. What does an introverted, unathletic writer-girl do with a Super Bowl afternoon? I had ventured outside familiar territory, and it turned out to be fun.

We're much too concerned about who we are. We're so protective of the image that others have of us. Well, others don't think about your image nearly as much as you do. So forget the "real" you today and have lunch with different people, or go buy a pair of funky shoes. Give up your perceptions of who you are, even if just for a day.

A Little Prayer for the Next Step

I need to loosen my grip on this image I have of "me." I need to forget about what's "good for me," what's a "good use of my time." I need to forget that I even have preferences or passions. Help me let go. Help me just experience life today, unhampered by my own ideas of who I am.

Act 10

TAKE A ROAD TRIP

*I feel so restless lately. The walls feel closer, and my days
are getting shorter. Maybe I'm the one getting smaller.
I have a good life, but it doesn't feel good right now.
What am I looking for?*

You're going to take a few hours off—or if you can, a day off.
You're going to pack some snacks and beverages and your favorite music. And you're going to put all of it in the car, fill up the
tank, and drive.

Just drive. Pick a direction; pick an area you don't know
much about. Or choose a route you enjoy but haven't been on
for a while. Drive and munch and listen and watch the scenery
go by. Feel the sensation of moving somewhere, of watching life
slide by your window.

The point of a road trip is twofold: (1) You get a change of
scenery, and (2) you confine your concerns to what you have
with you. The big rule of road trips is that you don't take work
with you. You can take along a hobby such as your photography

or journaling or drawing. But it can't feel like work; it must add to the adventure of the trip.

And if you can make it a longer trip—say, two days or a week—and include a friend or two, then the road trip gains real momentum in terms of getting you away and freshening up your view of the world. You can make it a theme trip. Make it a tour of small-town museums or of ballparks. I have some girlfriends who took a trip to explore diners in every town in the area.

If, like me, you live in a city with public transit, a train ride can be a decent substitute for a car trip. Take a transit line to the end and back again. Or get off the train at an interesting stop and wander around, then catch another train and continue the journey. A ride on public transportation is slower but cheaper, and although you can't take as much stuff with you, you can haul out a small backpack and roam with ease.

So make it an afternoon by yourself to no place specific or a days-long journey with friends and an agenda. But sometime soon, as soon as you can, do the road trip. Put on your comfortable shoes and leave your schedule behind. Look at how the sky and the land change, mile after mile.

A Little Prayer for the Next Step

Please open up the world to me, even if it's a small part of the world within a day's drive. Show me how to get new energy and new ideas from all the scenes and faces I pass. Help me stop and linger in the places that are good for my soul.

Acts of Daring

I was once told that if I am not failing *regularly*, I'm living so far below my potential that I'm failing anyway.

GREGG LEVOY, *CALLINGS*

Walk onto the Stage

Look to God

Make a Mess

Say Yes

Take a Little Walk with Jesus

Say a Prayer

Build on Hope

Face What You Dread

Say No

Say Good-Bye

WALK ONTO THE STAGE

*I know that I'm good at what I do, but somehow I can't
shake this feeling of weakness and incompetence. I don't
understand how such a lack of confidence can linger on,
even when I do well.*

It's time you were the center of attention. And it's important that
you're the center of attention in a way you usually aren't. Maybe
you lead a team of people at work, and so you're used to facilitat-
ing meetings. But you've never sung in front of people. Maybe
you're a performer in the arts, but you've never taken a group of
junior-high girls out for an afternoon of in-line skating.

You learn courage by putting yourself on stage. You learn
to think under pressure and to be gracious toward others even
while you're nervous and trying to concentrate. If you subject
yourself to this kind of pressure from time to time, then you'll
do just fine when center stage grabs you unexpectedly—and it

will. The key person won't be able to make a presentation, and you'll be left with the materials and a waiting audience. Or you'll find yourself in a situation of discouragement or panic when you are the person who is most senior or most experienced or with the most vested authority, and it will be up to you to help others ride out the crisis.

Sooner or later we have to stand up and do what others won't or can't do. We have to take extra responsibility, make important decisions on the fly, speak to an audience we never expected, or entertain the troops because the real act didn't show up.

So walk onto the stage. Put yourself out there and learn to sweat gracefully. Learn to deliver a coherent speech off the top of your head. It can be done, and you'll do it better if you give yourself opportunities to practice.

A Little Prayer for the Next Step

I'm going to do something that will make me really nervous, and if I bomb, a lot of people will witness the failure. Give me the grace and the guts to do it. Help me go through unexpected situations with kindness, good sense, and a supportive presence for others.

Act 12

LOOK TO GOD

I really need a place to open my soul—somewhere I can say everything I need to say and unload what's bothering me and what's making me happy. Sometimes I just feel full of stuff—good and bad—and have no place to put it and no good way to deal with it.

Sooner or later God figures in. It may happen when you finally stop struggling against all that is bigger than you. It may happen when you come to the end of your own resources. I've looked to God out of desperation, worry, anger, hope, happiness, excitement, and sorrow. I used to think that a person needed an agenda in order to look to God. But now I'm sure that some part of each person is simply made to relate to God; that God, in fact, created a space in your soul and mine just so we would not rest until we opened that space and said, "Welcome."

God is never what you expect. There's never the anger you've dreaded nor the approval you've longed for. Unlike human authority figures, God's primary concerns have to do with your well-being, not your performance. God celebrates you, the person created for a wonderful life, and God wants to help you participate fully in that celebration. God is the answer to questions you're still too dense to ask. God slips in at some weird moment and leaves you feeling like a happy idiot who doesn't even mind that she's an idiot but just loves being alive. Or God appears in the doorway and stands there until you face the one thing you've been avoiding, the thing that, once dealt with, will make your life go better.

So rather than waiting until you're forced by circumstances or angst to look to God, try looking to God just because it's good for your soul. Look to God when you think God isn't too pleased with how you're pushing your way through a situation, or when you're just tired and need comfort. Look to God when it occurs to you that you are surrounded by mystery.

Turning to God opens up the space in your soul that is waiting to be occupied. Looking to God is not complicated; it's a matter of stopping and saying, "Okay, I know you're out there. I know you're in here, too; otherwise I wouldn't even know to look for you. Help me see you, feel you, hear you, anything. Help me do what I need to do next. Help me find a golden moment or two in this next hour of my day."

A Little Prayer for the Next Step

What a wonderful thing that I am not alone! What a fantastic reality that there is a God who is interested in my life, who is rooting for me to make the right choice, to feel better, to live a worthwhile day. Thank you, thank you for being there.

Act 13

MAKE A MESS

*I've become so hyper lately, so obsessed with
details, so worried over things that even I know
don't matter. When did I get to be strung so tight?
How can I relax and enjoy life more?*

I can't remember a time when my grandmother's house wasn't
cluttered. She was always halfway through several projects.
Most of the time she had people in her house as well. Plus, she
liked to cook and make things for people. She knew where to
find whatever she needed, so her messiness never bothered me.
I knew that if I had to have scissors or green frosting, she'd
come through.

My house is cluttered too. I love stuff. I like to use it, orga-
nize it, look at it. I collect tea paraphernalia. I have books and
magazines all over the house. My husband is a photographer, so
we have his mess around as well.

When company comes, I straighten the mess. But I've learned to live with it. I say it's the sign of creativity. It's the evidence of happiness.

Be messy. Let your life's stuff hang out. Keep around you the things that make you happy. You could hire someone to deep clean the place every now and then, or you could clean house (or office) yourself. But don't mess with the mess. It keeps your interests close at hand. Don't put out of sight what gives you joy. Let the photos pile up on the countertop. It's nice if you can sort and display them, but until you have time for that, pile them. Leave your books and magazines all over the house. So what if you've started sixteen different books and articles? Bookmarks are inexpensive, especially if they are slips of newspaper or pieces of junk mail.

Mess is where life gets truly interesting. Don't be bothered by it unless it really gets in the way of your activity and creativity.

A Little Prayer for the Next Step

Please give me the discipline to get rid of the stuff that's not important, the freedom to savor the stuff that gives me joy, and the patience not to worry about the stuff that's messy but not hurting anybody.

Act 14
SAY YES

It's time for a change. It's time to make a decision to go
or to stay, to be involved or to disengage. The tension of
not doing anything is making me weird and irritating.

There's no feeling quite as giddy as the one that floods your being the moment you say yes to a big offer that's been handed to you. You say yes to marriage or yes to a new job. You say yes, in one way or another, to parenthood, or yes to volunteering your services in a strange environment.

Yes takes courage because yes is automatically a commitment. Yes means that you expect a decent performance out of yourself. When you say yes to the marriage proposal, you are assuming that you can be a good life partner to someone else. When you say yes to a new position in the work world, you assume that you will grow whatever skills you need to do the job. Yes is gutsy. Yes will stretch you clear out of your original shape. Yes will open up the world to you, one decision, one commitment at a time.

Think clearly—and then say yes. Dare to commit your developing skills and character to a worthy cause or calling.

A Little Prayer for the Next Step

Help me have the guts to say yes at the right times. And if I say yes, you'll help me fulfill that yes, won't you?

Act 15

TAKE A LITTLE WALK
WITH JESUS

*Why am I so argumentative lately? Why so
angry? And why am I frustrated to the bone
with where my life is going?*

Most of us like our independence; we try to thrive on our own
resources and intelligence. But we're really not designed for utter
self-sufficiency. We need other points of view. We need to hear
something besides our own voice talking.

You need help—but from whom? You're about as fed up
with the other people you know as you are with yourself. And,
please, not one more seminar or self-help guru.

Perhaps it's time to tap a resource much more timeless. In
the Christian tradition there's a spiritual practice of the imagination that can be very helpful when we're stuck. You simply
go to the Bible's New Testament, open up any of the Gospels
(the books of Matthew, Mark, Luke, or John), and read from the

many stories about Jesus of Nazareth. When you come upon a story that really intrigues you, read it again. Then read it again, only this time put yourself in that event, right alongside Jesus.

Imagine the situation, the conversations, how people move, their tones of voice, their gestures and facial expressions. Try to tap the emotions of the scene. And participate in that scene, as an onlooker or as one of the key players.

This may sound like just one more imaginative exercise, but it's a daring thing to put yourself in the same scene as Jesus. His teaching methods were unpredictable. And he could not be manipulated by others' thoughts or expectations. He said what he needed to say and did what he came to do. Hang around Jesus for very long, and who knows what will happen.

Get out of yourself today, and hit the road with Jesus. Be brave enough to hear his words, and allow yourself to be affected when he heals someone or probes with difficult questions into a person's soul.

I can't promise this little exercise will always feel sunny and easy, but it will definitely get you out of that rut of the self. Jesus has a way of moving us to healthy change.

A Little Prayer for the Next Step

Yes, I know that I often live in a very small world—that self-contained environment of my own opinions, wants, and hurts. I'm not too sure about walking with Jesus, but I'm willing to try. Help me get acquainted with him. Help me stay open to whatever I find in his story and his words.

Act 16

SAY A PRAYER

I know I need help that goes above and beyond what any person can give me. But I don't know how I feel about prayer. It seems presumptuous to ask favors of the Almighty. But I'm not sure what to do instead of praying.

It's fine to be open to God of the universe; it's a bit different to actually address God and expect any kind of response. You can be in the same room with your favorite movie star and just sort of bask in that star's presence—and that may be enough. But what if you walk up and introduce yourself? What then? In the same way, prayer is a crazy thing. It is a grand assumption that God cares for you in your singular life doing all the mundane things that make up a day. Prayer goes further than awareness. Prayer means that you put yourself out there very intentionally. You ask for help, for specific help, with something you need to do or a person you need to talk with or a wound that needs healing or a plan that needs to become clearer.

Walking up to God to say hello produces instant anxiety, at least at first. Once I learned that God is actually quite approachable, that God was, in fact, waiting for me to walk up and say hello, it became easier to drop whatever I was doing to say a prayer. In order to pray, I have to believe, at some level, that prayer makes a difference. It won't always make a difference in the circumstance, but it will nearly always make a difference inside me. Prayer is what happens when I know that I'm in over my head. Prayer is what happens when I'm so full of excitement or happiness that I have to share it with someone. Prayer can feel like sitting on the porch and talking with a good friend.

Saying a prayer will make a difference in this moment of this hour of this day. You take a risk in assuming that God of the universe takes notice of you. But in the very act of prayer, you find a renewed sense that God is present and waiting and full of good intentions for your soul.

A Little Prayer for the Next Step

Thank you, God, for being happy to see me walk up and introduce myself. Thank you for listening, for accepting who I am right now, even though I'm not perfect and I'm behind in my work and my soul has many rough edges. Thank you for the gift of conversation. I confess that I'll never know how prayer really works. But I trust that my words to you—no matter how bright or dark they are—are never wasted.

Act 17

BUILD ON HOPE

What a mess! If anything can go wrong, it will.
And people are looking to me to lead us out of all this.
We're all tired and discouraged, and no one feels like
coming up with an action plan.

Why don't you assume today that everything is going to turn
out all right? Your family, your work, your life calling, your
community—they're all heading in the right direction. Just
assume that.

Rather than trying to prepare for the worst possible sce-
nario, dare to build your day's words and actions on hope. Act
as if you expect people to do their jobs well. Act as if you expect
your kids will turn out all right. Act as if you know you will
do well and will love well the people in your life. Act as if your
community is becoming healthier, cleaner, wiser, and safer each
and every day.

We base so many of our actions and plans upon fears and
upon the prophecies of doomsayers. But those kinds of actions

and plans will never bloom into a hopeful future. So put away fear today. And build upon hope.

A Little Prayer for the Next Step

How much more positive my life would be if I just assumed that things will go well. Give me that kind of vision. Help me be hopeful in ways that are contagious to the people I deal with today.

Act 18

FACE WHAT YOU DREAD

I know that I should just deal with this thing that's causing me to lose sleep. I know what I have to do, but I'm just not ready for the stress. But this thing won't go away. I'm in knots from the minute I wake up in the morning.

Fear and dread are great cripplers of the spirit. I have been stopped cold by each of them on numerous occasions. They have prevented me from doing what I was called to do and have kept me from growing my gifts and my character. They have held me back in so many ways.

When you finally face the thing you fear or dread, it automatically becomes a smaller monster. The huge project becomes a series of smaller projects that you can actually do if you take them one at a time. The conversation you were sure would blow up in your face actually goes all right, and even if it doesn't, you vent or cry when it's over and then move on.

Whenever you experience inner resistance, there is a reason behind it. Maybe you've taken on more than you can manage. Maybe you must learn something, and you're not sure you can. Maybe you've placed very high stakes on this one thing, higher stakes than it deserves. Maybe you simply haven't thought through the consequences and so you have no plan and no back-up plan.

It's time to sit with yourself and ask, What am I so afraid of? What first step can I take to break free of this fear? What help from others do I need? Why is this so critical to my self-esteem?—and many other questions. It's time to face the person in you who is trying to run the opposite direction, to study the look on his face and figure out what all the fuss is about.

Take some time right now and have that conversation.

A Little Prayer for the Next Step

I need help. I need the wisdom to unpack this bag of fear and dread. Help me figure out what I am afraid of. Help me feel safe as I face that fear. I'm tired of not moving forward because of this stupid roadblock that's inside me. Give me the courage to learn the truth and go on from there.

Act 19
SAY NO

I just can't face this. I'm tired of being needed, tired of having too much to do. Most of all, I'm tired of feeling guilty for not doing everything that everybody "needs" me to do.

When you say no, you wipe out a lot of possibilities. That's why saying no is so scary. Maybe you really would make a good contribution to that organization. Maybe serving in this capacity today will open up a lot of other possibilities for you a year or two from now. You have no way of knowing that, but it is a worthy cause. It's easier to say yes than no.

It's difficult to say no to a good opportunity. It's more difficult to back out later and leave a vacuum, to admit that you should have said no in the first place.

Saying no applies to a lot of situations. You say no to turn down yet one more responsibility that you have no time for. But you also say no to people who are violating your personal boundaries. You say no when you disagree with a popular opinion. You say no when your child wants to do something you know isn't okay. You say no when someone is trying to go too far or push you too far.

No is a boundary, a limit, a cutoff, a safety precaution. No is good for us. No is necessary. No is also quite unpopular, because it always means someone is left unhappy. When you say no, you let people down, you disappoint them, you don't help out, you make someone mad, you introduce conflict. Saying no is extremely scary business.

But an honest and wise no is the right thing to say. An honest and wise no is just as powerful and good as any yes on any day.

Say no. Say it as gently as you need to. But make sure it is clearly understood.

A Little Prayer for the Next Step

This is so hard. I don't want to be a source of conflict or disappointment. But I know the right response on this issue is no. Just help me say it as graciously as possible.

Act 20

SAY GOOD-BYE

It's time to end this. I keep trying to make things stay the
way they've always been. But that doesn't work, and I'm
tired from trying. I guess it's time to say good-bye.

When a thing is over, good-bye is the only good response. Don't
make promises to stay in touch or to follow up. Don't try to
make this relationship more long-term than it's meant to be.
That sounds cold, but it's true; some relationships—whether
business or romance—are meant to be short-term, and to force
them to be anything else is merely painful and awkward.

And when good-bye means that the relationship is enter-
ing a new phase, acknowledge that change. You are saying
good-bye to the old phase. That coworker is moving across the
country, and she won't be your colleague in the office anymore.
But she will still be a colleague in the industry you both share,
and it's appropriate to stay in touch as colleagues, and even as
friends. Just don't expect the same level of relationship across this
new, very real distance. Your child is moving away to college or

getting married, and your relationship is about to change irrevo-cably. No longer will you be cued into the many activities and decisions of this son or daughter. You won't have the privilege of all those informal talks in the course of coming and going.

Say good-bye whether you'll miss the person or not, whether you like the person or not. Good-bye isn't about affection; it's about closure. For whatever reason, we need good-bye. It's a ritual that releases us from a present situation or relationship, and, generally, it is a mutual release. Saying good-bye shows respect for what has just ended, whether a partnership or a weekend retreat.

Say good-bye and let go. Trust that what has been done was good and that you have played a useful part in whatever is end-ing. Now you can move on with freedom.

A Little Prayer for the Next Step

I wish life were more permanent, that I didn't have to say good-bye so often. I especially want the good things to stay in my life. But someone always moves or something changes. Help me release my grip on the way things were. Help me say good-bye in a good spirit.

Acts of Generosity

Sure the world is full of trouble, but as long as we have
people undoing trouble we have a pretty good world.

HELEN KELLER

Give Praise Where It's Due

Help Someone

Lose an Argument

Listen to Someone Younger

Be the Bad Guy

Let an Opportunity Pass

Offer Forgiveness

Feed Somebody

Nurture a Colleague

Give a Friendly Push

Act 21

GIVE PRAISE
WHERE IT'S DUE

*I'm so tired of people looking weary and glum
wherever I go. Is everyone having that bad a day?
Am I stuck forever in this atmosphere?*

You'll be surprised at how people respond when you simply make the first move and say something nice. A courteous greeting will do, but a real compliment is even better. Most people try hard to do well. Sometimes their attempts are awkward and inadequate, and other times their effectiveness and success are astounding. Either way, it makes a big difference when one person walks up and says, "I really appreciate all your work."

Why be stingy with praise? Are we really so envious of another's success or giftedness that it hurts us to say "good job"? We train children from an early age to walk up to their opponents after a game and say, "Good game!" no matter who won. This attitude should travel with us every day.

I'm convinced of the virtue of giving praise because I have seen its effects so often. I don't gush or hand out empty compliments. But I have thanked janitors in public restrooms for keeping those places clean; I've complimented total strangers on their coats and hairdos. I've gone out of my way to tell some short-order cook that those were the best scrambled eggs I'd had in years. I'm not trying to earn points; I never expect to see these people again. But they've brought something good to my day, and they should be told about it.

We lose nothing by building up another person; we gain his look of surprised pleasure in response to our three-second statement. It's so easy to say thank you. It's quite effortless to tell a person that she's done a good job. And you can be fairly certain that your words will stand out to her in an ordinary day full of frustrations and complaints.

Before the day is over, find someone to praise.

A Little Prayer for the Next Step

Show me the people who are doing wonderful jobs. Point my genuine praise toward someone who really needs to hear it today.

HELP SOMEONE

There is too much pain and trouble in the world. Where does a person begin to make any difference? I tune in to the news and immediately feel helpless and hopeless.

Despite all the sarcastic remarks about do-gooders and the endless jokes about Boy Scouts helping folks across the street, helping others is what makes the world go round. For one thing, helping another person makes the helper feel good. We were designed to feel better when we cooperate. This is how societies hold together, how children get nurtured, and how victims of trouble make it through to better times.

Helping someone can be especially beneficial when you're becoming obsessed with your own situation. Sometimes you can't get out of your funk because all you can think about is how everything is not going well for you. The cardinal rule is that it's going even worse for someone else. You never have to look far to find a person in need of help.

Family members count, by the way. And they are quite touched when you stop and notice some way in which you can help out.

Neighbors count too. When you lend a hand, even in a small way, they will think of you truly as a neighbor, not just the person next door.

Strangers can offer us little blessings when we take the time to lend them a hand. You never know who that stranger will turn out to be (you know what they say about entertaining angels unawares), but it never hurts to be kind. And it can even be a good thing to help someone who is more grumpy than grateful for it. The point of helping is not to get thanked. It's to make the world a kinder place for a minute or two.

A Little Prayer for the Next Step

Show me who to help and how. Relieve my fears about how people might react. Remind me to say thanks for all the times I've been the recipient of someone else's help.

LOSE AN ARGUMENT

This conflict is wearing me out. Why can't we just agree? Why shouldn't I push through and not care about anybody's feelings? How do you resolve something that hangs on and feels so complicated?

It's an exhilarating thing to be proven right. It is deeply satisfying to be vindicated. Such exhilaration and satisfaction are the reasons people love to argue, why we hang on so long, why we *must* have the last word, and why we get red-faced and otherwise act like idiots over small matters.

Sometimes, though, there's something more important than being right. Sometimes the best thing is to be gracious, even humble. Maybe it's more valuable to let another person do something the wrong way and learn from it. Or maybe the argument is really another argument altogether, one that neither person can articulate, and so both people have chosen some other point to tussle over. Or—who knows?—you may be the one in the wrong, and the sooner you admit it and act like a good sport, the better everything will be.

Did you ever play tug of war when you were a kid, and you suddenly just let go and watched your opponent fall in surprise? Well, why not end an argument by suddenly saying, "You know, you're probably right. I'd rather that we get along and that you feel satisfied with the outcome. So let's do whatever you want. How can I help you achieve what you're aiming for?"

Such behavior can be a refreshing change of pace. Try it, or some version of it.

A Little Prayer for the Next Step

Help me be a big enough person to give in when giving in is the best thing to do. Help me look beyond this particular conflict to what is more important.

Act 24

LISTEN TO SOMEONE YOUNGER

I never thought I'd say this, but I fear that I'm already outliving my usefulness. I fear that people will stop listening to me or thinking that I have something to contribute.

Face it—you're getting older by the day. The good news is that, if you're paying attention to your life, you're also getting wiser. The bad news is that, little by little, you are growing out of touch with that sector of the population that moves fast and collects information and solves problems and makes decisions.

For everyone's sake, don't hold on to the past. One of the best ways to release your grip on it is to pay attention to someone a lot younger than you. Make a point to seek out a young person and ask questions, recruit abilities, and seek opinions.

If you find yourself in a meeting—whether it's business, church, or the local neighborhood organization—and you are part of that middle-aged or even senior-aged majority, make room for the younger members to speak up. Listen to what they say; you will learn something. You will also gain the friendship of people who have more energy and more time left than you do.

When you listen to younger people, you offer them respect and, thus, affirmation and encouragement. Listening is part of mentoring, but you don't have to be a mentor or have any sort of authority to listen.

A Little Prayer for the Next Step

How many people do I hang out with who are younger than me? Have I tried to protect myself from new ideas, from changing paradigms, from those people who will eventually replace me? Help me be more generous and open to the younger people who are coming up.

Act 25

BE THE BAD GUY

*A lot of damage is about to happen unless this problem
is dealt with in a constructive way. But I'm not the one in
authority. How can I help us come to resolution?*

Blame is a powerful antidote to pain, confusion, and anger.
When a horrible event takes the life of someone in the community, one of the first questions is, "Who did this?" When
an embarrassing error hurts an organization, it's not unusual
to see someone take the fall for it, whether or not that person
is actually to blame. Everyone feels better once the finger has
been pointed and some action has been taken. In a better world,
people wouldn't need such solace, but, in a perverse way, blame
helps us all get up and go on.

Usually more than one person is responsible when something goes wrong. In workplace situations, good supervisors
take responsibility for what has gone wrong in their depart-
ments. Correction may happen lower on the totem pole, but a
tone is set when someone steps forward. It creates the sense that

everyone understands what happened and that the thing is over now and we can all move forward.

It's not helpful to be the bad guy when you've had nothing to do with the problem. But if you're in the loop at all, consider giving everyone else a break and playing the bad guy today. Be the friend who messed up and didn't return the call; be the coworker who jammed up the process. If there's a way to take the pressure off others, do that sometime, maybe this very day. The truth is, others will understand that you aren't entirely to blame, and they probably won't stay mad at you, if they get mad at all. The point is to refocus everyone's attention on the next task, the next day.

A Little Prayer for the Next Step

I need to be honest, but I can be honest and still take the pressure off my friends, my family, and my coworkers. Blame is over-rated, and I can take a bit more than my share and not be hurt at all. Help me be the release valve. Help me do this wisely.

Act 26

LET AN OPPORTUNITY PASS

Somehow I've gotten into this pattern—certain jobs always go to me, and certain other people just grow more passive. It's not like I'm trying to be high profile or grab all the glory. But why am I the only one who volunteers for this or that? Why won't others speak up?

This situation develops a lot in churches and other volunteer communities. It also appears sometimes in the workplace, where stronger personalities will accrue more and more responsibility while those who are quieter or less confident shrink back. Two dynamics are at work here: you are on your way to burnout, and others are shying away from their gifts and abilities. Perhaps you have more status, or more seniority, or a more assertive personality. Who knows how these patterns develop? It's rarely the doing of one person. But often it takes just one person to change the direction of things.

This time—and maybe for the next few times—let that opportunity pass you by. Of course you are capable of performing that task or service. Of course you would do a great job. But let it go anyway. Create a vacancy in the system that someone else must fill. This will be difficult, because people have come to expect certain things from you. And the vacancy may stay vacant long enough to cause people discomfort.

But the generous, balanced thing to do is step back so that others may step forward. The Christian Scriptures refer to people as various parts of one body, with each having his or her gifts to offer to the whole community. Yet we often don't function as though this were true. It takes true generosity of spirit to allow your own voice or influence to decrease so that someone else's may better flourish.

A Little Prayer for the Next Step

Why am I so hesitant to step back, to give up status or influence? What is this need I have to grab every opportunity to prove myself or be useful? I really want to grow in generosity—it makes for a much healthier world. Help me release my grip so that others can get a better one.

Act 27

OFFER FORGIVENESS

*This is never going to be resolved to my satisfaction.
The other person won't see it my way, and I
won't see it any other way—that's just the way it
is. But we still have to live in the world together.
I can't take this emotional upheaval anymore.*

Forgiveness is the solution to situations that have no solution. When nothing else can be done, when everything has failed, gotten too complicated, and left a bad taste in your mouth, forgiveness is the one final step you can take.

Forgiveness is an act of letting go. It's required for long-term relationships, for the effective ends of wars, and for heavy-duty healing.

Forgiveness is *not* what you do when someone has inconvenienced you, momentarily hurt your feelings, or broken your taillight. Unless you're really petty, you can get over those ordinary, irritating moments that visit us so often.

No, forgiveness is for hurt that is deep and bitter and inescapable. It's what you do when the confusion over who said or did what just keeps getting more confusing. When you can't forget about it, make up as if nothing happened, or apply all those principles of conflict resolution, all that's left is to let go and say, "I don't understand why you've done this to me, and I don't excuse it, but I forgive you, and it's time to move beyond this."

Jesus Christ was very big on forgiveness, one reason he stuck in the craw of a lot of rigid, play-by-the-rules people. Forgiveness is what you apply when the rules are broken beyond repair.

Today may be the day you need to offer forgiveness for wrongs—past or present, committed by loved ones or enemies—that won't let you sleep or enjoy anything anymore. Often, when I say the Lord's Prayer and come to the part about forgiving those who sin against me, I insert the names of a few people. These people have hurt me deeply, and I continue to practice forgiveness and will do so until the healing is complete. So I insert those names, in that way stating my intention to really forgive these people. It's a small step, but I go forward.

Forgiveness begins when you simply decide to do it. It hardly ever happens all at once, but if you decide today that you will offer forgiveness, you are well on your way to healing.

A Little Prayer for the Next Step

Forgiveness does not fit any system that makes sense, so I need help. Help me say, "I forgive you, if only in my mind." Help me say it out loud if that's what needs to happen. Help me say it as many times as I need to, until it's true.

Act 28

FEED SOMEBODY

*I'd really like to do something for this person,
but I don't want to make it a big production or
make the person feel obligated to me.*

Some of us have grown up in families that show people love by feeding them. To be cooked for, to have the plate piled high, or to have a package of homemade baked goods appear on the doorstep is to be nurtured and remembered.

Want to make someone feel better immediately? Buy her coffee; put a treat in his mail slot at work; knock on her door with a fresh pot of soup; send a box of assorted edible things that will keep, such as bean-soup packages, candy, little crackers, tea or coffee packets, and tiny rounds of cheese.

Make dinner for a family that's been struck by illness or some other trial. Pick up some carry-out food and go visit the new parents who are tired and will not have a social life for several months.

We were designed in such a way that we must eat every day; thus, there are many opportunities to help folks meet this ordinary need. Feed someone. The recipient will feel cared for, and you will experience a spike in happiness.

A Little Prayer for the Next Step

How basic can you get? I can do this kind of nurture any way I want—a little gift, a dinner, something homemade or that I pick up from the grocery store. Help me be alert to who might like this sort of creative kindness.

NURTURE A COLLEAGUE

There's got to be more to my job than just doing my job. There must be something I can do that goes beyond this project and my life. Unfortunately, I don't know much about any other skills or jobs.

Healthy competition keeps us all moving and stretching. But cooperation is just as important.

Walk around your workplace and look at the people there. Or if you work at home or have your own business, take a tour of people who are your peers, whether they are stay-at-home parents, freelance photographers, or truck drivers. Take the time to look at faces and listen to voices. Someone you know is struggling at his or her work. Maybe he's exhausted, or maybe she's run into a snag and can't find a solution yet. He might need to hear about someone else's difficulty with a project, and she might need the benefit of someone else's experience. One person needs help networking, and another just needs a few minutes of supportive company.

Whoever you are, you have something to offer. Decide what that is and be the best nurturer you can be. Look for a way to help another person be successful. It won't cost you anything to build up another person's confidence or address book. Generous people get taken advantage of sometimes, but that's no excuse to stop being generous.

Help the whole world step forward today by nurturing a person in his or her work.

A Little Prayer for the Next Step

Forgive me for being so defensive of my own position that I don't reach out more naturally and more often. Show me the person who could benefit today, this week, this month, from my experience, my sense of humor, my contacts, or my insight.

Act 30

GIVE A FRIENDLY PUSH

This friend really needs to make a move. She (or he) has been in this situation way too long for it to be healthy.

You've been there. You knew that you should make an appointment to see the doctor, or that it was time to get a reliable car, or that life would improve immediately if you had the strength to end a bad relationship. But these forward movements were difficult to make. You faced both internal and external resistance.

Then someone who truly cared about you gave you a kick and said, "Do it!" It was exactly what you needed, and you finally did what needed to be done. When it was over, you thanked the person whose footprint was still on your backside.

It could be a big thing, such as finding a more suitable living situation, or a small thing, such as getting new glasses, but someone you know could use a little push. If you're his or her boss, you're in a good position to nudge. But you don't have to have authority to give a friendly kick; you simply have to care.

Nudge someone who is too tired or too hesitant to make that healthy move. Take care not to be pushy or to be a therapist. All this person needs is someone's permission to do what is already clear. Maybe all it will take is looking up a phone number or doing something else to help the research along.

When I cut back to a part-time editing schedule, I announced my intention to get a dog. I'd wanted one for years, and my husband and I had agreed that once I was home more, it would be okay to have a pet in the house. So I started talking about it shortly after my work schedule changed. We would go to a local shelter and rescue a dog. I planned out loud when I thought we'd do this. Then I would hesitate when I remembered how much trouble a dog can be. But I knew that eventually I'd get a dog.

Then my office mates gave me gift certificates to PETCO. That was all the push I needed. They had invested real cash in my dog-to-be. So within a couple of weeks, I had the dog and had spent all the certificates. Of course, this puppy was lots of trouble! But she's affectionate and is my buddy whether I'm writing or playing. I'm glad I finally took that step.

Do the loving thing and help someone overcome personal inertia.

A Little Prayer for the Next Step

I need to pay better attention so that I notice when someone needs a friendly push. Show me what I can offer to *do*; I don't want to simply stand by, waiting to be asked for my opinion or my help. I don't want to be too pushy or make another person's decision for him or her either. Point me toward the balance.

Acts of Healing

Tending the things around us and becoming sensitive
to the importance of home, daily schedule, and maybe
even the clothes we wear, are ways of caring for
the soul.

THOMAS MOORE, *CARE OF THE SOUL*

Take a Walk
Choose Not to Care
Remember Other Pilgrims
Daydream
Shut Off the Information
Tell Someone Your Troubles
Learn to Do Nothing
Cry
Get Quiet
Relive Good Times

Act 31

TAKE A WALK

I am going crazy. If I don't do something in the next five minutes to change my life, I'll just blow up!

If this is how you feel, then you need to move around a little. It's surprising what a difference physical movement can make in an otherwise abstract, stuck day. It's as if the mind were made to be in a moving vehicle. Some people run or swim or lift weights or play team sports. Any of these will work. I walk because I am not athletic, and to become athletic would be a stressful experience all by itself. I need physical movement for its *release* of stress.

You can probably walk more in the course of an ordinary workday. You can walk during a break, or you can walk the dog. You walk in order to take deep breaths or to mutter at your day, to give your mind roaming room or to think of nothing at all. You might walk with a coworker or friend, or you might walk in order to be alone for a few moments.

Walking moves you out of a stale space and puts you in contact with sounds and scenery that wake up your senses. Walking relieves the physical tension that builds up when you've had to hunker over a computer half the day or sit in a meeting for two hours.

So before you blow up or visit the vending machine one more time, take a walk. Leave your environment for ten minutes. Swing your arms and breathe deeply as you go.

A Little Prayer for the Next Step

If I take the moments to walk, will you bring me a breath of fresh air? If I move to a new space for a while, will you make it interesting and help my mind break out of its patterns? If I take time to look at clouds or flowers, will you fill my creative self with a new idea or two?

Act 32

CHOOSE NOT TO CARE

*I have too many things on my plate. I'm going to burn
out very soon if something doesn't change.*

Sometimes you have to give yourself permission to just not care
so much about how something will turn out. I work on words
for a living, and with each book I edit I must come to a point
where I am willing to let go of a manuscript and allow its process toward publication to continue. There will always be more
to do. And sometimes I would fix one or two more things that
need fixing if only there were another week. But I can't afford
another week. I have to not care quite so much about making
this project the work of art I had envisioned.

It's all right not to care about some things. If you care
deeply about everything, you'll never be able to rest. If you take
responsibility for everything, you'll rob others of the opportunity to act, and you'll keep yourself up nights over matters that

71

don't really matter. Everything isn't up to you—it really isn't. The world won't end if something for which you're responsible doesn't turn out perfectly. People won't even remember what might have turned out better if only you had spent a little more time on it or done one more thing.

The truth is, it's up to you to prioritize all the jobs and tasks in your life. You can decide what is most important, what is next in importance, what you can take or leave, and what has nothing to do with you. Others may think you should care, but it's not their job to decide what your priorities should be. In making good decisions, you save for the world your best self and conserve for the best projects your prime energy.

So if you are overwhelmed, find one thing to stop caring about and stop caring right now.

A Little Prayer for the Next Step

The world will just have to keep on going, even though I'm not going to move any further with this. I know you know that other things are more deserving of my concern. I'm just one person, and I will give myself to the task that is most important right now. Thank you for understanding my limits and for helping me understand them. Help me deal with the people who won't.

Act 33

REMEMBER
OTHER PILGRIMS

*Sometimes I feel as if I'm ruining everything. I'm not
grown up enough to live my life. I'm not wise enough or
strong enough or kind enough. What can I do?*

It's good to remember that someone has already lived a life that
is quite similar to the one you're living. Someone before you was
the mother of three children under the age of eight. Someone
else succeeded at a task that seemed impossible at first. Someone
else faced cancer or financial reversal or divorce or the violent
death of a loved one. Someone else failed at one or more careers
before discovering her true gifts and callings.

You're not the only pilgrim on this path. Many have jour-
neyed ahead of you. So when toils and troubles become overwhelming, find a spot at the roadside and sit for a while and
remember those other pilgrims. Ask yourself, What would

she have done? or How did he handle this when it happened to him?

You may have to go looking for the stories that will help you. That could mean spending an hour or so with some elderly relative or church member and asking questions such as "How did you manage having teenagers in the house as well as your seventy-year-old mother?" or "What did it take for you to leave that career?" Some of the best pilgrim stories are the lives of the saints, available through many books and films. Some pilgrims are your contemporaries, and other pilgrims live on through their stories alone, which are preserved through books, movies, or simply the memories of others.

And sometimes all you really need to remember is what your own parents went through. As I've become more of a grownup, my mother has told me more about her own sorrows and difficulties—as well as her answered prayers and small miracles. When I see what she has survived and what a strong, kind person she now is, I feel a bit more confident that I will get through whatever is on the road today.

A Little Prayer for the Next Step

I am surrounded by the stories of other people, but I need to pay better attention. Help me gain strength and hope from all those other pilgrims on the path, not only the ones traveling alongside me today, but those who have passed this way before.

Act 34

DAYDREAM

*I have so much to get done today, but my head's not in
it. My mind just keeps wandering when I need to focus!*

It's time for a daydream. Go all out. Win the Nobel Prize or an
Oscar, pick up a handsome stranger, make a speech in front of
thousands, and relive that disagreement—only this time think of
the right thing to say at the right time. Let your mind do what
the real you can't do right now.

The imagination is a spiritual function. Any true faith
requires imagination because, at some point, you must be able
to envision what you believe. I grew up being told that fantasies
were bad, which probably set my creativity back a few years.
Daydreams are little exercises, that's all. They are pressure valves
that allow you to feel good about your life or to laugh at yourself
even when you're in the midst of an uninspiring, stuck-feeling
day. Sometimes all you need to get through the present hour is
to imagine the end of the day and a warm bed. Other situations
require a more specific vision, such as what this project will look

like when you've finally completed it. Give yourself permission to jump forward in time and daydream about being successful at something that is full of trials right now. Learn to exercise your imagination in constructive ways.

Give in to your mind's tendency to escape. It wants to escape for a reason. You're piling up too much pressure somewhere. Or maybe you're simply tired. Close the blinds, shut the door, and spend five or ten minutes imagining the thing that could take you away from all of this. It will, in fact, take you away for a few moments. Then you can come back, feeling silly and refreshed, and get your work done.

A Little Prayer for the Next Step

I don't know why I'm so afraid of my imagination sometimes. It's part of my life that you've designed to help me. So I'll give myself permission to daydream. Show me how to use this gift.

Act 35

SHUT OFF THE INFORMATION

*It's scary not to have any control over how
stressed I feel. And the stress spreads itself over
every part of my life; it seems as if every minute
I'm worried about something else.*

You receive more information in a day than your great-grandmother received in a month. Think about that. In a few seconds you can know what is happening to people far from here whom you will never meet personally. If you watch television news, listen to radio, read newspapers and magazines, and surf the Internet, then you are constantly absorbing much more information than you have the ability to deal with.

You may understand a lot of details about many of the world's problems. But there is only so much you can do with your one life during this hour or day. So relieve yourself of information. Don't listen to the news today. Leave the newspaper alone. Don't go online. Take a break from information. After a point it is no longer information, but merely more noise in your head.

Your mind and soul need breathing space. They can't always be solving problems or forming opinions. You can't be constantly reacting emotionally to a half-dozen events at a time. You were never meant to carry such burdens.

Close the door to information today. The world will keep on its tumultuous way. When you are able and it's time, you will find the precise information you need in order to do what needs to be done.

A Little Prayer for the Next Step

God, deliver me from the addiction to information. Give me the wisdom to choose when and what to know, to learn, and to respond to. I'm grateful that you will not hold me responsible for everything that happens in the world.

Act 36

TELL SOMEONE
YOUR TROUBLES

It would feel so good to be heard and understood for a change. But here I am, same as always, dealing with everyone else's problems. I want to be a friend to other people, but what do I do with all the hurt and frustration that keep welling up in my own soul?

When you must verbalize your hurts, fears, and frustrations, find a good listener. We've known people who made a daily habit of telling others their troubles—and we've run the other direction when we saw them coming. You won't become that kind of person just because you need a listening ear from time to time.

You do this sort of processing for a specific reason, with a specific person, at a specific time. Some people go to a pastor or therapist when they need to unload. For others, a close friend will do. A child might use a favorite toy or the family dog.

Maybe your grandmother who lives five states away can offer you a listener's healing by way of an old-fashioned telephone call.

Don't underestimate the healing that comes from merely being heard. I did much better at dealing with conflicts in my marriage once I started talking to some of my married women friends. I found out that I wasn't alone. I learned to stop worrying so much about conflicts that I discovered were common to most marriages. I was able to take the pressure off both my husband and me. I even learned to laugh at some of my frustrations—but only after I had laughed about those frustrations with other women who were going through the same thing. Telling my troubles helped my marriage more than I ever expected.

The people around us, even those closest to us, are dealing with their own situations, so you can't assume that another person is going to catch the hint when you make a passing reference about your loneliness, anger, or fatigue. If you need to talk, be direct about it. When you are full to the brim with a difficult situation, find the right person to help shoulder the load. Allow someone else to look at your life, assess the damage or the promise, or reflect your own wisdom back to you. This is a worthy exercise. When one person listens—really listens—to another, the help will come.

A Little Prayer for the Next Step

Show me the right person, place, and time for this. I know that I try to hold everything inside and just deal with it myself. I keep forgetting that life is a journey we take with other people. Give me the help I need through a person who knows how to listen.

Act 37

LEARN TO DO NOTHING

I am trapped in a cycle of weariness and worry.
I don't know what to do with this.

I think it's no accident that some people experience a sort of conversion after they have had to spend extended time in a hospital bed or on sick leave. When we're very ill or critically injured, we are forced to a helpless stillness that most of us never learn otherwise. We want to solve our problems, get on with life, come up with a plan, get moving again. But suddenly we are weak and immobile, and all that's left to do is be where we are and take no action whatsoever.

And sometimes that's exactly what we need—to come to a complete stop. In 1521, a young Ignatius of Loyola lost his military career when a cannonball shattered his leg. He nearly lost his leg and his life, but a long convalescence spared both. While he was resting and healing and facing the fact that life as he'd known it was over, his deeper self embarked on a season of reflection, discernment, and self-discovery. By the time he could walk again, he was on a new road altogether—to dedicate his life to God and, eventually, help found the Society of Jesus, commonly known as the order of the Jesuits. The interior process he discovered, beginning with those months of "doing nothing," he later explored more fully and wrote up in his Spiritual Exercises, which are now used around the world to help people with spiritual growth and discernment.

While you may not be on the cusp of a complete life change—maybe all you really need is a few days of rest—don't underestimate how important it is to truly stop the action in your life. When you can learn to do nothing but simply be, your interior life has the opportunity to make its own sort of progress. Most of us are so frenetically busy that we cannot hear our own souls talking to us, warning us away from unhealthy attitudes or asking for some quiet hours in which to recuperate.

If you're weary and stressed, take a day (at least) to do nothing at all. Sometimes in order to go forward a person has to stand still and let the real motion begin.

A Little Prayer for the Next Step

All right, I thought I knew how to take a break, but there must be more to understand about resting and holding still. Help me to stop trying to fix things or come up with better plans. Help me stay still and not do anything but allow your life and health to fill me.

Act 38
CRY

*I'm sad, but I don't know why. Pent-up
emotion won't quite come to the surface.
It just makes me stressed and gloomy.*

There are a couple of movies on my DVD shelf that I keep for
the express purpose of bringing on a good cry. I keep certain
musical selections for the same reason. Because life is so constant
and demanding, we become expert at saving our emotions until
we have more time and space for them. This is especially true
of the emotions that lead to tears. So when I'm feeling particu-
larly pent-up, on the verge of tears but unable to really deliver,
I prime the pump.

Tears happen because we need them. They offer a unique
cleansing to both body and soul. It is a system of release that
apparently is not present in any other species. Somehow, human
emotion, which is connected to the deep ever-after soul, is also
connected to the very pragmatic physical systems that keep out
infection, regulate body temperature, fill and empty the lungs,

and pump the blood. Tears are proof that we are indeed whole persons in whom the physical and spiritual merge.

We cry in response to physical pain, disappointment, frustration, anger, sadness, humor, ecstasy, and grief. Our tears know how we feel sometimes before our brains do. Our tears know when we've had enough already.

Make sure that you have provided space in your life for tears of every kind. They heal in more ways than you know. Even if you have to put on sad music to get the process going, do so without shame. Don't wait for a good reason to cry; cry because you want to. If you want to, that probably means you need to. Cry in private or with company. Cry naked in the shower before your day begins or bundled up on a garden bench in midwinter. Listen to your body and let the tears flow.

A Little Prayer for the Next Step

I don't know why I'm embarrassed to cry. Why should anyone feel wrong about something so natural and so necessary to health and peace of mind? Help me release emotion in a way that brings healing.

Act 39

GET QUIET

Please, everything must stop!
I can't breathe or think or do anything.

Just outside my hometown in southeast Kansas is a single hill created decades ago by coal mining. It's wedged between railroad property and soybean fields, and over the years trees and bushes have grown up on it. It's not a high hill, but when I was a kid, I used to ride my bike to its base and then climb to the top. From there I could feel the breeze and watch field hawks wheel over the crops. Mostly I liked it because it was completely quiet up there. I could sit and do nothing at all.

I live in a city now, and I find quiet spots on the lakefront not far from my home. When weather or time does not permit that outing, I go to the bedroom and shut the door. There's no radio or television in the bedroom. I've learned to keep noise out of that room because sometimes a person just needs to be quiet and be surrounded by quiet.

Getting quiet is not the same as praying. It's the cessation of your own noise, even the inner noise. Maybe you pray in order to get quiet, but the point is to empty your life of the clatter.

In the middle of your workday, shut the door or, if you're a cube person, go to a spot that is traffic-free. Sit on that back step that no one else uses. Or go to the smokers' area when smokers aren't there. Sit in the sun and suspend thinking for a few minutes.

Learn where the quiet places are. They may be in churches and libraries, but then again they may not be. They could be in neglected corners of parks or inconveniently placed offices or restrooms in a workplace that are not used frequently.

Turn off the radio, the television, your iPod, and the feature on your computer that tells you you've got mail. Sit in the quiet until you can actually feel the quiet. Close your eyes or focus on something that doesn't represent stress.

Most important, once you have found or created quiet, do not then fill it up with your own noise. Quiet time is for stilling the soul, not revving it up by concentrating on tasks or problems.

A Little Prayer for the Next Step

God, I'm not sure I can find or create true quiet. Show me one place this week where I can still my mind and heart.

RELIVE GOOD TIMES

I wish I could be more hopeful about the future, but mostly I worry about it. Sometimes I even fear it. I'd like to learn how to be more hopeful and positive. Nothing makes me feel so stuck as constant negativity.

It's important to store up good memories and then dust them off from time to time. Take photos, run the video camera, save mementos, or write events in a journal. Sometimes I keep a scrapbook. Mostly I stuff programs, photos, and ticket stubs into the bookcase to be found later, much later, possibly months from now, when I finally clean the bookcase. Then I find the stash, and all cleaning stops while I look at all my stuff and reminisce.

The book of Psalms in the Bible—in fact, much of the Old Testament—contains many examples of people reliving better times. While in exile or being pursued by enemies, they would recall the glory days when God had delivered them and when the blessings flowed freely.

A good memory relived can be almost as good as the event itself. And sometimes your experience in the years since can lend more meaning to the event when you look back at it.

Keep in mind that, in God's realm, everything is present tense. God is not subject to space and time. And so your past is, in fact, a piece of your present. Even though it's past, it is still a real part of you. The good times do count, even decades later.

Unlock your inner closets and drawers and boxes and take out those good times. The emotions from those times will return as well, like sudden whiffs of perfume from an old scarf in the attic. In this way your memories can bring healing to the times that aren't so happy.

Good times of the past are evidence that good times do happen—and that they will probably happen again.

A Little Prayer for the Next Step

I tend to forget all those gifts I have—the treasures I keep confined to something I call the past. They are still mine. They can't be taken away. Even if my own memory fails, whatever trinkets remain, whatever remembrances others carry, keep the good times alive. Help me exercise my memory often.

Acts of Integrity

When we first come to [God], we try . . . to be some other person that we think we are supposed to be. But the more we get to know him, the more we discover that he has created us to be ourselves. And we discover this not all at once, but little by little.

EMILIE GRIFFIN, *TURNING*

Identify That Feeling

Admit Defeat

Ask for Help

Tell the Truth

Confess Your Faults

Forgive Yourself

Listen to a Critic

Uncover Your Attachments

Grieve the Loss

Look in the Mirror

Act 41

IDENTIFY THAT
FEELING

Why do people treat me as if they're afraid I'll bite their head off? Why do I feel so out of control? I've not actually done anything wrong or inappropriate. But I'm becoming a person who makes others uncomfortable.

The true emotions of a typical day wear very odd disguises. You might be angry, but you express frustration or hurt feelings. You might be sad, but it comes out in complaint form. Grief becomes distraction; anxiety turns into hyperactivity.

Well, most of the people in your world today will pick up on the *actual* emotion. They will hear you say you're not angry, just tired, but they will *feel* the impact of your *anger*. Emotions are like that—they issue from the intuitive self and are read quite clearly by the intuition of others.

If someone accuses you of being mad or depressed or tired, don't answer right away. Try to suspend your defensive reply and follow up by asking, "What makes you think that?" Then listen to the answer. Let others reflect to you what your body, tone of voice, and eyes are telling the world. Thank people for their observations. Then go somewhere and shut the door.

Dare to consider that you really are what people are seeing. Look in the mirror at your face, your posture. What's looking back at you? How do you really feel?

Once you've identified the feeling, you can dig around for the reason. When you've figured out the reason, your options will open up. You will decide to have an overdue conversation with someone or to go to bed earlier tonight. Because you faced your emotional life with honesty, the rest of your life can get back on track.

A Little Prayer for the Next Step

Why am I so afraid of my own feelings? What do I think will happen if I see them for what they are? Please deliver me from the idea that feelings make me weak or stupid. Help me use emotions as they come—to build wisdom.

Act 42

ADMIT DEFEAT

This thing is too screwed up to be fixed.
I would give anything to just be rid of it.

It's time to give up. It's not in your nature to give up. You're a responsible person, and people rely on you. But, for whatever reason, this thing you were determined to do—and do well—is not turning out well. And you cannot make it turn out well. You can't fix it. You can't even figure out why it needs to be fixed. You don't know what to do. You don't have the tools or you don't have the time or you don't have the inner resources to follow through, carry on, pull it off, keep it up, or make it to the end. You wish you could have done it. You know that some people will be disappointed. You're disappointed too.

Why expend a lot more energy getting nowhere? You've proven through the years that your energy can do good for a lot of other projects. So you'll figure out whom you need to inform and to whom you need to apologize and how to pack it up and say good-bye. And rather than feel guilty for weeks, you'll simply say this: I failed. I'm sorry.

Many of us have to admit that we entered the wrong profession. I enjoyed teaching music in public schools, but after only two years I knew it was not a good fit for me in the long run. I wouldn't say I failed as a teacher, but to stay in that career would have been a mistake. Quitting that profession meant an entire college degree would be of no further use to me. For a few years I kept a teaching certificate valid in one state or another, but finally I let that go too.

That's it. Don't let this situation go on and on. Admit defeat and free yourself.

A Little Prayer for the Next Step

I failed. You know I didn't mean to. You know that I really did care and try hard. I don't know why I couldn't do it, but you do. I'm sorry about this. But failure is part of moving forward, of learning my strengths and weaknesses. So I'm letting this go now and calling it the failure it is. Let's talk later about what comes next.

Act 43
ASK FOR HELP

I can't face this thing that I need to do. I'm doing
everything in my power to avoid it altogether. But,
of course, I'm stuck with it and must finish it, and
I can't move anywhere else until it's done.

There comes a time when you have to admit that you can't do it alone. You don't have the information or the skill or the time or the will. Yet you keep hanging on to the task, thinking that you can force progress. Well, progress doesn't respond to force. It's time to ask for help.

It's true that if you need to ask for help *all* the time, then it may be time to change your situation—volunteer for something else or get another job. But most of us need assistance sometimes.

The key to asking for help is to figure out what kind of help you need. Do you need enough feedback on this project to move ahead with confidence? Do you need better information from someone? Do you need to work out a different schedule for doing this task? Do you simply need another warm body around to help you juggle all the tasks involved? Once you know what you really need, you can go to your supervisor, or whomever else, and ask in a pleasant, direct way for real help.

What you don't want to do is wait until you've already missed the deadline or until you're so overwhelmed that you can hardly get out of bed in the morning. Then what you're asking for is not help, but damage control. No one—especially a supervisor—likes damage control, but he or she is usually happy to give help.

Years ago I took an editorial position at a new company. When I attended my first editorial lunch, a regular meeting at which editors talked about work and life in general, I let it slip that I was taking work home almost nightly. When our editorial director heard that, he explained what I should do when a project was slipping behind and how asking for help early was better than getting overwhelmed down the line. Another editor, a woman who had been there a few years, said to me, "Vinita, look in the mirror and repeat this to yourself: 'I am not Jesus.'" Everyone at the table burst into laughter at that bit of advice, but I have remembered it ever since.

It's good to remind yourself that you do not have superpowers. Drop whatever else you're doing, and figure out what kind of help you need—then ask for it.

A Little Prayer for the Next Step
I don't even know what help I should ask for. Help!

Act 44
TELL THE TRUTH

I'm worn out from trying to make myself look good
to the whole world. I'm tired of trying to stay in
everyone's good graces. I need a clean slate.
I just want to give up every pretense and live my life.

Tell the truth from the very beginning. Or if you didn't start out with the truth, jump back to it at the first opportunity. A lie requires better memory than the truth, and sooner or later memory fails some detail in the lie, and you're found out.

Tell the truth when you've messed up. Tell the truth when someone asks your opinion—although you should ask, before giving your opinion, if that is what the person truly wants. Tell the truth about the little things—the fact that you forgot an appointment rather than got caught in traffic. (Maybe you did get caught in traffic, but it was forgetting the appointment that made you late.) The small lie that lets you off the hook makes it easier next time to doctor facts for the sake of your image. Admit you're forgetful or that you didn't do what you said you would in the time frame you promised. Most people overcommit themselves and then are tempted to lie in order to free themselves. All of us wear out and don't finish things sometimes.

Tell the truth, but with love. Sometimes honesty will cause pain to a loved one. How do you know if you're speaking the truth in love? Ask yourself, *Is it satisfying to say what I'm saying, or is it difficult and painful to say it?* If telling the truth is an excuse to tell someone off or to vent your own emotions, that's not love. If speaking the truth is the last thing you want to do because you know it will sting, you're probably speaking out of love. Say what needs to be said, but clothe it in all the empathy and understanding you can.

The truth is the only story that lines up correctly with the universe. It won't always be pleasant, but it will keep you in harmony with life in general. And your reputation for honesty will carry you past many hurts that result from truthfulness.

A Little Prayer for the Next Step

I don't have the energy to spin lies, little or otherwise. I want to live honestly, wisely, kindly. Help me recognize when I'm wandering from the true story.

Act 45

CONFESS
YOUR FAULTS

I'm carrying a weight I can't get rid of.
There's so much to make up for, and
I'll never be able to undo what I've done.

I've noticed that when I confess to someone how I've messed up, most of the time the person releases me from guilt almost immediately. It's as if he or she is so grateful that I've owned up to the problem, the offense itself isn't so horrible. And once the issue is out in the open, the tension dissipates—the tension inside me as well as whatever tension was lingering between me and the other person.

The Christian church has a history of confession practices. In some denominations it's quite a formal process; in others it's "share time." But all those folks have figured out that confession is good for the soul.

Sometimes you let people down. Sometimes you say and do things that are hurtful. Sometimes you do harm to yourself. We often call it *sin*. It does exist, this tendency to do the wrong thing, sometimes with the best of intentions.

When you've done something wrong, the simplest solution is to confess. That's not to say that it's easy. Sometimes you'd rather die than confess. But confession helps. Maybe you need to confess to a person you've wronged, or maybe you just need to put into words, for yourself, what you've done. A lot of people find great comfort in confessing to God or to a priest.

On the job, it's better to confess than to cover your tracks. Tracks don't cover that easily, and it will look ten times worse if you're found out later. Most supervisors and vice presidents trust a person who is honest about his or her mistakes. They appreciate it when you have enough integrity to step forward. They're even more impressed when you express remorse and explain how you'll avoid making that mistake again.

Confession is, most of all, about honesty. It isn't a ploy to get people to like you (and they won't anyway if you confess but just turn around and repeat the offense). It's not a way to earn brownie points in heaven, no matter how many people treat it as such. Confession is your opportunity to do right even when you've done wrong.

A Little Prayer for the Next Step

I need courage today—to confess my fault, my sin, my weakness, my guilt. Show me how.

FORGIVE YOURSELF

*I can't look forward to things in a positive way anymore
because deep down I know that I'm never really up to
the task. I've failed so many times already.*

You will always be harder on yourself than you are on anyone else. You may be mad at your sister for several months over some holiday incident. But the anger you keep simmering in that pot on the back of the stove—that's just for you.

Yes, you blew that opportunity. You didn't handle that conflict very well. You cramped the relationship with your expectations. You pushed the child too hard. You didn't eat right. You made a bad financial decision. You wasted time. You didn't take the risk. You threw away a perfectly good job.

You didn't do enough. You didn't try hard enough. You acted like an idiot. You forgot the most important things.

Yes, you did all of that. And although you will keep growing and maturing, you'll also keep messing up; you'll just find new forms and means for it.

Years ago I read *Ordinary People,* a novel by Judith Guest. The main character is a suicidal boy named Conrad. He and his brother had been in a boating accident, in which the brother died. Throughout the story it is clear that Conrad and his mother cannot communicate and that she carries a lot of anger. But the real turning point occurs when Conrad realizes that he's the one who is unable to offer himself forgiveness—for surviving the accident and then for subjecting his family to a bloody suicide attempt. Guest's story illustrates vividly how we struggle to forgive ourselves, sometimes even when we're not at fault.

Have you wronged another person or God? There's nothing left but to ask God for forgiveness and keep walking. You may need to ask someone else for forgiveness as well. And don't forget to forgive yourself. It's the only way to keep trying, giving, thinking, doing, and being. Are you carrying guilt that doesn't even belong to you? Find a way to look at the situation truthfully so you can let yourself off the hook.

And when all of this seems too difficult to accomplish, ask God for help. Forgiveness is an act of the soul, and it needs spiritual reinforcement.

A Little Prayer for the Next Step

I am so, so sorry, so full of regret. There's no point in trying to take it all apart and figure out why or why not. Help me get over this. Help me cut myself some slack. I generally forgive other people when they ask for mercy—why is it so hard to be that gracious to myself? Help me understand what forgiveness is and what it means that you forgive me, so that I'm able to move on.

Act 47

LISTEN TO A CRITIC

I've taken my work as far as I can, but I'd like someone else's feedback. I know I'll never be objective enough to judge my own work well. But I'm afraid of criticism that's harmful. How do I go about getting the help I need?

As a writer, I have learned the value of others' input. It hardly ever feels good to be critiqued thoroughly, but my writing craft would be in sad shape without it.

Good criticism is valuable information. When someone gives constructive criticism, he or she offers you a wider view of something that is visible to you only in close-up pieces.

Keep in mind, though, that you shouldn't ask anyone's opinion of your work unless you really want to know. And when you do ask, be ready to take notes.

The key to getting good criticism is asking for it in the right way. Be specific about the kind of feedback you need. When I ask people to react to my writing, I make specific requests. Maybe I ask them to comment on the craft itself—the word choice, the technical aspects of the work. Or I ask for a general emotional response to the writing—the atmosphere it creates, the feel of it. When I'm at early draft stage, I don't want anyone's opinion of sentence structure and word choice; I'm not at that point yet. I'm more interested in whether or not the reader connects emotionally to the idea or excerpt.

When something about your work bothers another person, find out why. Chances are that this person's not the only one who's bothered. Solicit the opinions of people whose opinions really count. When it comes to workplace issues, a supervisor's opinion counts more than your husband's. When you're at an advanced stage with a painting, you go to an expert for help, not another student. Be sensible when you ask for criticism.

In the end, it's up to you to evaluate others' evaluations of you. But your own evaluation isn't much good until you decide to listen to what others have to say.

A Little Prayer for the Next Step

Help me to be secure enough in what I do that I am encouraged, not deflated, when others find ways to improve it.

Act 48

UNCOVER YOUR ATTACHMENTS

*I don't know why it's so difficult for me to do the things
I consider most important. There's always something
getting in the way. I'll see what I want to do but not
have the inner strength or commitment to do it.*

The main person getting in your way is often you. Humans tend
to carry around their own competing agendas. Sometimes, what
rules us is nothing more than an unhealthy attachment.

- Yes, you want to try something new. However, you
  can't let go of the need to be safe, and new experiences
  come with no guarantees.
- Yes, you want to give more—time or money—to a worthy cause. However, you must have a certain amount of
  money in the bank in order to feel secure. So, of course
  you can't pass up the overtime hours.

- Yes, you want to be your best self in this relationship. However, you also want the relationship to move in a certain direction, and quickly, because you don't want to be alone. So the self you bring to the relationship is too needy and pushes too hard for what it wants.
- Yes, you are convinced that the policy (at work or in Congress) must be questioned. However, there's job security to consider. Also, you don't want to come across as some loopy radical—you need for people to think well of you.

This list is endless. You (or I) can't move forward because of unhealthy attachments. We need this or want that. We must be comfortable or stay in a position of power. We cannot relinquish what little control we think we have. In fact, our attachments are so strong that they get in the way of making good decisions. Rather than living out our intentions in clear choices, we are moved this way and that by our fears and egotistical motivations.

So, what are your attachments? What is paralyzing you? What is pushing you? Once you figure that out, you'll be better able to live the life you really want.

A Little Prayer for the Next Step

This is really tough. I didn't realize how so much of my life is influenced by these nearly hidden fears and obsessions. Please help me sort out what is either holding me back or pushing me in the wrong direction.

Act 49

GRIEVE THE LOSS

*There is so much hurt in my life right now that nothing
works. I can't think clearly or even feel things in a normal
way. It's as if I have a wall on every side of me, and
I can't move the wall or get around it.*

Everything blew up in your face. When the smoke cleared, you
found a lot of your possessions busted up or gone altogether. The
relationship was over. The project was killed. The dream was
dead. The loved one was gone.

How can you do anything now? How can you even breathe
or think? Everything has changed. You are lost, and you have
lost what is important to you. Your life will never go back to
what it was.

You know that it's time to cry. It's time to moan and scream
and sit in that deadly silence and stay up all night and not eat
a thing. It's time to grieve. One of these days you will make
plans again. You'll gather the pieces that are left and figure out
what you might do. One of these days you might even imagine

a future. But not now. And it's unfair for anyone to expect that now. You don't owe anyone an explanation. You don't care about what they think. They either get it or they don't.

You will grieve until the comfort comes. You will do what you can do, which isn't much. It may not be much for a long time.

It's time to give yourself permission to grieve. So do whatever you feel is necessary to make some space in your life right now for the grieving.

When my father died and then when I lost my only pregnancy, I learned that grief has a life of its own, and that the cycles of mourning must be respected. Those cycles are inside you, and they help you know when it's time to cry, to reminisce, to thank God for the good things, and to surrender to God all those painful, unanswered questions.

A Little Prayer for the Next Step

One comfort I have is knowing that you understand how weak and empty I am right now. Thank you for not expecting much. Thank you for absorbing my shrieks of sorrow and rage. Please, please hold on to me.

LOOK IN THE MIRROR

*This sounds strange, but I don't feel connected to
my own life. Some days I have no good sense
of who I am or what I'm trying to do. It's as if
I'm fragmented and can't pull myself together.*

Mirrors are quite useful if you know how to use them. Here's a
simple exercise.

Look in the mirror and note the following:

- How's your posture? Are you tired, hesitant, defensive?
  Or are you confident, relaxed, purposeful?
- What do your eyes say? Do you see fear, self-loathing,
  lack of sleep, anxiety? Or hopefulness, contentment, a
  well-rested psyche?
- Is your face a pleasant place? Even if it's wrinkled and
  marked, does it have that sheen of softness, a kind glow,
  a readiness to smile or laugh? Or does it carry a record
  of only the bad events and memories?

- Is your hair a wreck? Have you conditioned and trimmed it lately? Or is life actually so busy you can't stop for an hour of decent grooming? Does it shine, does it speak well of your life?
- Observe your clothes. What do they say about you?

All right. Record the results. You don't have to show them to anyone. But you do have to make the assessment. No one else in this world will ever take responsibility for the story told by your mirror.

A Little Prayer for the Next Step

I probably look for the wrong things in that mirror. I try to see the person I'm not rather than face the person I am. Help me look with steady eyes at that person. Show me how to care for her better.

Acts of Joy

The soul of one who loves God always swims in joy, always keeps holiday, and is always in the mood for singing.

St. John of the Cross

Sing a Song
Watch Children or Animals
Congratulate Yourself
Play in the Dirt
Allow Some Happiness
Do the Spa
Attend the Feast
Laugh Out Loud
Give Worship a Try
Throw a Little Party

Act 51

SING A SONG

*Something inside me feels light today, as if my soul
needs to bounce around the room. I feel restless, but
I can't think of any way to relieve it.*

Music is a great gift to us. We should use it a lot—in fact, it should be part of each day. For centuries people of faith and substance have sung to God every day, some of them several times a day. Music is soul language; it reaches us in ways we will never be able to explain or appreciate fully.

In the midst of a hectic day, it can be good to drop everything long enough to sing a song. It's easy to merely listen to a song, especially if you're in the habit of turning on the radio. But it's even better to sing. When you sing you're exercising a part of yourself that doesn't get much attention, and you air out the dull, toneless self that forgets how good it is to dance. In fact, even better than singing a song is dancing your own little dance. Best of all is to sing and dance at the same time.

I used to sing a lot when my business was music. I hardly sing at all anymore, but I've developed the habit of memorizing certain songs that are easy for me to sing to myself as I'm walking. They make good use of what voice I have left, and they are generally positive songs that shore up what I believe about life.

Of course, a person can't always burst into song in the middle of a board meeting. (Well, now that I think about it, would it hurt that much?) But there's always someplace you can sneak to for a few moments to sing your little song. It can be a prayer song or a stupid song or a nostalgic song or a totally made-up-off-the-top-of-your-head song. Doesn't matter if it doesn't make much sense. It especially doesn't matter if you can't carry a tune. The real singing happens inside; the physical singing merely helps the inside voice to wake up and make some noise.

Sing for no reason at all except to take a break and give yourself a lift.

A Little Prayer for the Next Step

Help me sing often and with much gusto.

Act 52

WATCH CHILDREN OR ANIMALS

I'd love to just go have fun today. But there's too much work to do, and I can't find a babysitter. I'm tired of television. What I'd give for a good laugh right now.

If you really want to commit an act of sheer joy, turn a small child and a puppy loose in the same room. Their play is absolute. Their discoveries are ecstatic. Their joy will disarm you. Even their disagreements have an element of fun.

A few years ago, I adopted a dog from the shelter. And I must say that I play more now, at midlife, than I did decades ago. My joyful play is also due partly to having a next-door neighbor with a little girl. With the help of the child and the dog, I have discovered a pure form of joy; it's called play. It's easy to forget how to play when you work for a paycheck and take responsibility for a household. But play and joy are joined at the heart.

So even if you are unable physically to play with the child or the animal, sit and watch them. For that matter, watch children on the playground, a toddler discovering leaves, otters at the zoo, squirrels running along the electric lines. There's joyful drama happening right in your neighborhood under your nose. When you lose a sense of joy, look to the creatures that are not self-conscious and consumed by their own plans.

A Little Prayer for the Next Step
Give me the ability to learn from the little ones and animals how to play and be joyful.

Act 53

CONGRATULATE
YOURSELF

*You'd think that after the success of my last endeavor
I would feel better than this. I should be able to
go on to the next thing, more confident than ever.
But I can't seem to get moving. What's wrong with me?*

No matter how much work is waiting for me and how many ideas I have for new writing ventures, I am unable to start a new project immediately after I've completed a project. Something inside me resists pushing on to the next thing right away. For some reason, my soul needs some breathing time before starting a new creative work. And it doesn't seem right to begin a new work if I have not fully appreciated my accomplishment of the one that came before. So I have learned to make time for rest and for self-congratulation before resuming work. When I finish a manuscript or even a specific stage of a manuscript, I take a break from writing, and I no longer feel guilty about that.

If you've completed a stage of work or accomplished a difficult job, that's cause for celebration. Stop long enough to congratulate yourself in a tangible way. Go celebrate!

I celebrate by inviting a friend out for lunch or coffee. I celebrate by looking at my accomplishment in solitude and smiling broadly to myself. I celebrate by picking up the phone and telling somebody about it. I celebrate by sleeping in the next day or by going out to eat at a fancier place than usual.

Others may notice what you've done well, but no one else will understand what it took to pull it off. You're the only one who can recall the details, the long hours, the frustrations and troubleshooting. You have earned praise, but no one else can praise you fully enough.

So treat yourself the way you would treat any other person who's done a good job. Find a way to celebrate. Raise your glass of iced tea and make a toast to your own job well done.

A Little Prayer for the Next Step

Thank you for helping me do things well. I couldn't have done it without a lot of help. You gave me the resources, the strength, the support of other people. You looked on with pleasure while I did what needed to be done. Please remind me of this moment the next time I'm deep into something that seems endless and impossible.

PLAY IN THE DIRT

I don't know how to play anymore. And most games require other people. How can I loosen up on my own?

A few years ago, my husband and I took our granddaughter camping. In this particular state park is a creek, and about a mile up the creek the banks are sheer clay. Kids wade there to slide down the slick banks and paint themselves and one another with the shiny wet stuff. So six-year-old Alexis and I waded up the creek and spent nearly an hour playing in clay. We were in bathing suits and so had lots of skin to paint. The only problem was that by the time we waded back to the lakefront, the temperature had dropped and Alexis was already shivering, so we didn't wash off in the lake as planned. We walked all the way back to the campground looking like extras from some movie about aliens or zombies.

The globe is so covered with dirt that we must be meant to get into it. Children know this instinctively. Some adults hang on to the instinct by becoming gardeners of one sort or another. Others like to tramp around in the woods and come home sprinkled with the evidence of a day in the country—those pungent smells and traces of nature's grime.

You may know the Bible verse that says from dust we came and to dust we will return. But you don't have to die to get back in touch with your physiological roots. You can sit in a nearby park—on the ground, not a bench—and play with the grass, the leaves, the sticks, the sand, the mud, the loam. Smell it, rub it between your fingers, look closely at its color. Just sit there for a while.

Or be the gardener and immerse yourself in dirt, hours per week. Come in gritty and happy and watch those earth tones run down the shower drain. Dirt is good for you. Its scent does something deep in your soul. Its covering is good for the skin. And it can feel like so many different things when you touch it—every temperature and every state of aridity or gooeyness. It's stuff that gives you life, real stuff that we try to avoid way too much.

Play in the dirt, for a few minutes at least. Allow yourself to remember that childhood happiness of making mud pies or smearing clay in kooky designs down your arms and legs.

A Little Prayer for the Next Step

Help me play more often and not shy away from things I think are childish or messy. Show me some nice dirt to play with for a while.

Act 55

ALLOW SOME HAPPINESS

Sometimes I think I'm immune to happiness.
Something always gets in the way of my feeling
really good about life. What is wrong with me?
Will I ever get out of this rut?

It's hard to be happy. There's so much standing in the way. For one thing, after every happy event something bad is bound to happen. We all know this. We know that if we're too happy for too long, then we'll surely pay for it eventually.

So we guard against happiness. We try to ration it out, to temper it with plenty of soberness and worry. This is a sensible, balanced way to live. Don't be too happy for too long. Then no one will notice and try to snatch that happiness from you.

Such a sorry lot we are. There are no rules for happiness. There is no quota that we must be careful of lest we set our own little universe out of kilter. Our happiness does not make God angry or anxious. God would love it if we'd just relax and enjoy ourselves more.

I am finally learning that I need to stop regularly and ask myself what is standing in the way of feeling good this very moment. When I search for anything specific, I usually come up empty. And, no longer having an excuse to be unhappy, I enjoy life the way I should have been enjoying it all along.

If a happy moment comes your way, exploit it fully. Don't let anything fill its space—no worries, no apologies, no contingency plans, and no guilt.

You indulge fully in misery, don't you? Try giving happiness equal time.

A Little Prayer for the Next Step

Okay, okay, I'll allow the happiness to come right in. I won't try to make it leave early. I'll enjoy it to the hilt.

Act 56

DO THE SPA

*When will someone take care of me for a change?
I spend my days taking care of everybody else. Or
I spend most of my time working. Even vacations
turn into work. I want to feel totally relaxed for
a change. I want to pay attention to myself
without feeling guilty or self-indulgent.*

I finally decided, during my forties, to give my body intentional time on a regular basis. I developed some simple habits that have been good for this body, such as soaking in a bathtub regularly, or taking a short nap after arriving home from work. It doesn't cost a fortune to fill a room with relaxing scents, and it's surprisingly simple to massage my own aching limbs and joints. Every now and then, I pay someone to give me a real massage, which does wonders for a body that spends hours per day at a computer. These activities used to feel like luxuries, but I've learned to respect the body for the hard worker it is. And now I'm kinder to mine.

There are full-blown spas that cost a lot of money and provide everything from nutritional plans to exercise regimens. There are less intense retreats where you can soak in a hot tub and get a good massage. Then there's your own bathroom, with a lock on the door, a candle or two, and mineral salts or scented oil. You can add music, food and drink, and reading material. My husband and I have recently discovered the glory of resting in a hammock under the shade tree, which for some reason is even more relaxing than lying on a bed—probably has something to do with birds and breezes.

Being joyful by way of the spa means that you do whatever it takes to help your physical self feel happy and at ease. Your spa may include a sweaty workout, a long hike, a new haircut, a body wrapped in herbs and mud, an afternoon lying in sand and sun (or shade), or an entire morning of making love.

Listen to your body and learn what it wants and needs. Give it a few hours off—or at least part of an hour, during which you ignore everything else. Aim for fifteen minutes every day during which your body can be completely relaxed. Fifteen minutes is possible on almost any day—think of how many quarter hours get squandered on television or checking e-mail one more time. This physical self carries your soul ceaselessly through every minute, all your life. Be nice to it. Give it some joy.

A Little Prayer for the Next Step

I offer to you my body as it is. Give me wisdom to care for it joyfully.

Act 57

ATTEND THE FEAST

I'm hungry all the time—and for all the wrong things.
My cravings have become my prison. I can't get
through a day without all this angst about food.
Feeding my body shouldn't be so stressful.

It's not easy to enjoy good food. We know too much about it—
how many fat grams we can consume without guilt, how much
fish or soy we should have, and what kinds of vegetables give us
the best nutrition for our buck.

For the sake of your joy today, forget about all that. Attend
a feast where every dish is a work of art, prepared for the sake
of sheer pleasure. Eat slowly, course by course, taking the time
to converse happily with the people at your table. Feasting is an
activity that should always involve good company, unchecked
laughter, and friendly lighting.

A feast doesn't have to be a huge production. Sometimes an
evening of soup and bread, shared with loved ones, is the best
feast of all. But a true feast is a form of celebration. It doesn't

make people nervous or self-conscious. There aren't any rules or quotas to worry about. A feast feeds both the body and the soul, in the company of people who are good for you.

Find a feast and attend it with joy. Or make your own feast and invite someone you care about. He or she probably needs a feast too.

A Little Prayer for the Next Step

Oh, thank you for good things to eat. Thank you for good people who can sit around the table with me. Teach me the art of feasting.

Act 58

LAUGH OUT LOUD

I just feel crazy today, in a good way.
But the world isn't kind to craziness, and
I don't know how to work off this energy.

I confess that I love to laugh, that I laugh easily, and that I don't care what I sound like when I laugh. I am unfamiliar with any concept that censors laughter. I laugh when something strikes me as funny, and occasionally people around me don't think I'm being appropriate. But you can't help what tickles the funny bone.

When you laugh, you exercise your body. When you laugh, you provide release for positive energy. Sometimes you provide release for negative energy, and the laughter turns to tears, which means you needed to cry anyway.

My husband and I both suffer from chronic depression. We have learned over the years to gather a collection of funny movies and comic performances, and sometimes after dinner, we play one and just exercise the laughing part of our personalities.

We also read to each other, everything from humor columns to goofy e-mail jokes. This has helped us through some pretty dark times.

But laughter is primarily an expression of joy. It's a natural response to the wonderful discoveries we make as we walk through the world.

Go through the rest of this day pretending you are in the middle of a feature-length comedy. Look for the gags and punch lines occurring naturally all around you. And laugh as loudly and as long as you want.

A Little Prayer for the Next Step

I want to laugh, I really do. And I don't want to have to work at it, either. Just help me have some fun.

Act 59

GIVE WORSHIP A TRY

*Why is it so hard to relax and breathe? Why do I feel
so bound up, so tense? I need a release valve of some
kind. I need to sing or cry or something.*

Entertain this thought: You were designed to connect to a
Higher Power. No matter what you call the Higher Power, your
very soul desires connection with that entity. This is the way it's
always been, and through the centuries people have come up
with various ways to connect with their God. Worship is one of
those ways, and it continues in every culture and era. Perhaps
we should pay attention to a spiritual practice that has remained
in place so consistently.

Authentic worship provides the release valve for emotions,
desires, and soul expression in general. Are you grateful for
all the gifts in your life? Join in the singing of hymns. Are
you burdened with guilt over what you've done or failed to
do? Take advantage of those time-tested prayers of confession.
Do you need help? Add your prayers to the many others being

voiced or thought during the worship or prayer service. Do you want to walk out into your week, encouraged to be your best self and to do amazing work in the world? Allow sermons, Scriptures, prayers, liturgies, and conversations to fuel your life for the days ahead.

Much that's called "worship" is anything but—it is stale, lifeless, depressing, and static. So, find the worship out there that is real—and be assured that such worship does exist. When we make connection with and express our souls to God, joy is always involved, even if it accompanies confession or healing or desperate prayer. The connection itself energizes life, and this is joy at its most elemental.

Go all out. Sing some praise. Kneel and pray. Look another person in the eye and speak a blessing. If you're stuck, healthy worship will get you moving again. It is impossible to connect with Divine life and not be changed.

A Little Prayer for the Next Step

To be honest, I've not experienced much worship that seemed to be true connection with God. But I'm willing to keep looking. Help me learn what it means to sing and pray and listen and move.

Act 60

THROW A LITTLE PARTY

Why doesn't anyone know how to have fun anymore?
If this is what it means to be a grownup, then let me be
a kid again. I need to party!

So throw a little party. Or throw a big party, if that's fun for you. For many people, a big party means big stress, and a party is supposed to be a joyous activity. I happen to derive great joy from studying recipes, planning a menu, cooking for days ahead of time and then feeding more people than can fit around my table. But that's me—a person for whom cooking holds inherent joy.

You may not even like to cook, so work around that part of it. Have every person bring a dish or have everyone kick in a few bucks and order pizza. Maybe you love games or chips and dip in front of the television at play-off time. Or maybe a party for you is sitting with friends at a local gathering place or going with girlfriends to some hotel that offers a full afternoon tea service. Two people can make a very fine party. Maybe a party for you is wearing something nice and bringing ice cream, a bowl, and two spoons to the bed that you've shared with this other person for years.

Whatever is a party for you, make it happen. Life is short and full of toil and trouble—as poets and prophets have said—and we must make parties from time to time just to ensure that we practice the joyful part of ourselves.

Do not wait for an excuse to have a party. Do not assume that a good party is one that involves printed invitations or is planned weeks in advance. Some of the best parties happen when two or three people decide to have fun for an afternoon or evening rather than go home and deal with the normal chores.

Enjoy your life. Don't wait until circumstances get better. Don't put off parties until you're not so tired or don't have as many responsibilities. Throw a party simply to celebrate the blessings and graces that are in your life right now. When you celebrate you communicate that, even in tough times, you believe life is good and the future is worth waiting for.

A Little Prayer for the Next Step

Forgive me for not partying enough. There is so much to celebrate—maybe not a lot of big things, but certainly many small, wonderful things, every day. Help me become a person for whom celebration is a way of life.

EPILOGUE

You may have noticed by now that the acts in this book don't require great intellect or spiritual insight. A lot of them are pretty simple. They may even make you feel silly. You've been doing some of them all along without realizing how wise you were.

But please remember: Everything matters. All the small steps you take are in one direction or another. What you do during the few minutes you are waiting in line can actually make a difference to you and to the people waiting with you.

You're an important person. What you say and do has an impact on all sorts of people you don't even know. You can make the world better just by your presence, your smile, or a word or two offered at the right time.

You're a person worthy of wonder. Most of your gifts are yet undiscovered. I hope that practicing some of the little acts in this book will help you discover the hidden parts of you that are so amazing and so good for the world.

Take that step. Lean forward into your future. Enjoy the journey!

ABOUT THE AUTHOR

VINITA HAMPTON WRIGHT has been a book editor for nearly two decades and a retreat/workshop leader for eight years. Her most recent novel, *Dwelling Places,* won the Christianity Today award for Best Fiction of 2007. Her nonfiction books include *The Soul Tells a Story: Engaging Creativity with Spirituality in the Writing Life; A Catalogue of Angels; The St. Thérèse of Lisieux Prayer Book;* and *Days of Deepening Friendship: For the Woman Who Wants Authentic Life with God.* Ms. Wright lives in Chicago with her husband, Jim Wright.

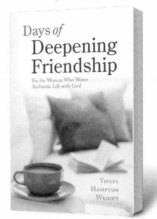